CW00520797

BBC Slam Champion, Jess Green is
script writer for theatre, TV and poc
at Glastonbury, Latitude and BBC 6
taken her 5* shows, Burning Books
Being In Love With Jeremy Corbyn
and on national tours. She has featured on BBC 6 Music, E4,
BBC5Live, ITV and BBC Breakfast as well as in The Guardian,
Huffington Post, The Independent and The Spectator. She's
written for EastEnders, Holby City and Casualty as well as a
poem for Eurovision 2023.

Dressed as Love

Jess Green

Illustrated by Rosie Johnson

Burning Eye

BurningEyeBooks
Never Knowingly
Mainstream

This edition published by Burning Eye Books 2023

www.burningeye.co.uk

@burningeyebooks

Burning Eye Books
15 West Hill, Portishead, BS20 6LG

ISBN 978-1-913958-44-2

For me at thirteen.
Hang in there, girl.

Contents

there's a whole lot more where that came from

Things to Remember During My Autumn of Rejections

I'm the naked toddler in the living room
screaming for everyone to watch the
dance routine I've been doing all holiday
and clap like it's *King Lear* at the Globe.

I'm at the teacher's desk
holding a rock I found on Dad's allotment
carried into school in kitchen towel,
the remains of a Roman emperor, probably.
She tells me to sit down,
stop wasting everyone's time.
I scoff she'll be sorry
when this is in the British Museum
and I'm a millionaire.

My World War I poem
mounted on red card
three weeks on the classroom wall
until it's taken down
because I find my fame too distracting.

The job interview I'm invited to attend
when the *Evington Echo*
publish my article about Greek cork farmers.
I arrive in dungarees.
They suggest ten is too young
for a career in journalism
and I say,

But there's a whole lot more
where that came from.

It's Him

The man at work who bought you
a Zadie Smith hardback in the Secret Santa
always restocks the teabags
when it's not his turn.

He did a 5k dressed as a pirate
for children with cancer.
Everyone cheered him over the finish line,
then laughed at the photos
passed round the office on Monday.

He runs the Woodcraft Summer Camp,
drives the bus, lights the fire,
turns a blind eye to teenage tent drinking.

Has pictures of his kids
on his desk on a beach
in sun hats.

He's got a blue tick on Twitter,
retweets opinion pieces
on the MeToo campaign,
says he hopes his employees know
they can always come to him.

He baked a round of brownies
for Staff Bake Off,
won first prize,
donated the plastic medal
to the lady who came second.

His wife's delightful,
head of marketing
at a local theatre.
She smiled at you once in Sainsbury's
beside their daughter holding
a Peppa Pig magazine.

They host garden parties in summer.
He does a bulk buy from Majestic Wines,
invites the women from the office,
spends the evening mentioning French films he likes.

He speaks a lot.
Gets in there first whenever your name's brought up.

📍 15 km away

Keen runner, sometimes
run for charity but no biggie.
Just trying to do my bit.

📍 15 km away

Being at one with nature. My
happy place.
Something about the air and
the trees.

📍 15 km away

Star Baker...
Joking, I promise it's just a
hobby.
Never take myself too
seriously.

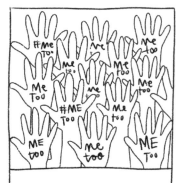

📍 15 km away

I will ALWAYS be an ally.

EVIDENCE BAG

EVIDENCE BAG

EVIDENCE BAG

EVIDENCE BAG

EVIDENCE BAG

EVIDENCE BAG

Keep Your Engine Running Knowing Full Well the World Is Burning

I used to think that adults meant safety
with their people carriers and thick jumpers.

Adults went sofa shopping,
organised barbecues,
bought nice yoghurts,
had clean towels
and good pyjamas.

I couldn't wait for it,
to get past the stage of wanting
to chop my own hands off
if I didn't have pockets.

I'd walk around with my arms crossed
at the same time
that men began telling me
to cheer up.

At parties I was desperate for grown-ups,
scoured the room during pass the parcel
for someone who could intervene
at the first sign of cheating.

I'd slip out of sleepovers to sit on the carpet
next to mums watching ITV crime dramas.
You couldn't be homesick
when you were pressed against a faux leather
three-piece suite and Inspector Barnaby
was about to make an arrest.

If I got lost as a toddler
I knew to approach the first woman I met,
show her the number scrawled up my arm
and ask her to phone home.

I longed for adults,
the ones who did big shops,
had golden retrievers,
hosted dinner parties,
cooked Ottolenghi recipes,
had neck rests on their office chairs,
blankets across the back seats of their Volvos.

I wanted adults with routines and boring jobs,
adults who noticed the thirteen-year-old girl
on the carpet beside them
while everyone else was next door
doing Ouija boards.

Now I pay my mortgage each month
and think
look at you pretending,

spend bank holidays
in DFS combing the crowds for a mother
who might take me home,
so we can watch *Midsomer Murders* together.

Hey, Kiddo

he arrives dressed as love
you're in pigtails and a bucket hat
with no change for the payphone

he's your father
doctor
bartender

half-price pints
lock-in for your mates
lift home at the end of the night

he's got deep pockets
a smile like a rock in a storm

where do you want to go?
a boot full of booze
enough weed to keep you high for a month

he stops in country roads
weighs his confidence by the tonne
watches you in the passenger seat
offers to give you some

Hell to Pay

Bikini handstands,
teenage skin
greasy with sun cream.

Across the sand he shouts my name,
swaggering Brit Abroad,
sunburn and beer gut.

They've got jetskis.

He points to the jetty at the end of the beach.
The girls look at me.
I sink.

He's impatient.
None of us speak.
Emma grabs my hand –

She already promised to go on with me!

– we run, fast as we can. He's behind us, like he's in on the
joke. We know he'll grab us if he catches up. Emma fumbles
with her money case, throws a few coins at the vendor who
tries to show us how to start the engine –

– he's coming up the jetty now, so I get on. Her behind me. I
press a lever and we shoot forward. She holds tight round my
waist. He's shouting from the shore. I glance, can't help but
laugh. We keep going. Until we can't hear him.

Then stop.

She rests her cheek against my back,
water slap against plastic;

our breath catches.

Blue Skies and Service Stations

I knock on his mum's room
after lights out and tell her what he does to me
back home.

We look at each other in our nightdresses.
She says she'll deal with it,
sends me to bed with the other girls
and I sleep with my eyes on the door.

Next morning she appears mother hen
in a polyester skirt,
herding stale-cider children
with the air of someone
who just delivered a fatal blow.

I am cartwheeling safety.
The bus opens with a piston.
Tonight I will eat pizza with my friends
in some evening square
on this council-funded trip across Italy.
Next week I will be in school
with a canister of film
in the Kodak kiosk.

I crouch down to change the CD on my Walkman,
notice my bag's not in the hold.

It waits on the tarmac.

He picks it up,
puts it on the back seat of his car
with the air of someone
who just received a fatal blow.

Family Dinners

like a McCain's chips advert
sturdy hugs and Sunday jumpers
no one gets a word in
over all the conversation
a bike left propped
against a picket fence

a dog in a basket
hasn't shat on the floor
no toddler has stood in it
no sibling drums their fingers
at news of their sister's extension
a song through the Alexa speaker
that noughties David Gray hit
reminds the father of a holiday
in southern Spain
he tells the story of the grapes
and the waiter again
everyone laughs

there's cake
nobody grits their teeth
nothing is said in hushed tones
over washing up

before they leave
they make a date
to do it again

knowing that no one will cancel
last minute.

Was It the Same on the Accountancy Course?

she dyed her hair like a tequila sunrise
worked minimum wage on the Liverpool ghost tour
arrived at the pub for last orders
dressed as a dead woman

her voice too loud for the lecture hall
she turned round in *Waiting for Godot*
shouted, *what a load of shit!*

wore a half-knitted jumper for graduation
determined to finish it before they said her name
stumbled across the stage
needles hanging from a sleeve

he had eyes for her the moment she walked in
all mouth and colour
a wake of chaos wherever she went

after they slept together
he called her Sylvia
put a hand on her shoulder
whenever she spoke

It Wasn't a Party

Let's not make something of nothing.
He's a hard-working guy
leading us through a pandemic.
There are gonna be times he needed to kick back
with some cheese and wine,
games and quizzes,
pin the tail on the care home worker.
How many people died alone over a six-week period?
Multiple choice;
do you want a clue?
Hancock got it.
'Course he did.
But let's not blow this out of proportion.
What's a few festivities between
MPs, journalists and the Met police?
You couldn't all be invited.
Someone had to keep A&E going,
staff vaccination centres,
comfort the children
when they turned off Mum's ventilator.

Look, he's sorry if you've decided to be offended.
Is it gaslighting
or is it you being oversensitive?
Here's a picture of him with another one of his kids.
How can you stay mad at this
fun guy,
drunk uncle,
bumbling dad at a wedding;
how many has he had?
He's Les Dawson,
Bernard Manning,
he was only kidding.
Have another drink.
There's enough cocaine for everyone.
Let's not talk about mass graves
and overflowing ICU wards now,
mood killer.

We all work hard,
just some of us a little harder than others.
You can't complain.
You had your Zoom funerals,
Rishi payouts;
don't say we never give you anything.
Sure, it's a shame that your business went under,
but a little of Daddy's investment
a contract for your mate who owns the local pub
will set you back on your feet.

He knows it was tough,
but at times wasn't it quaint?
In your cosy homes,
cladded high rises,
turkey for one
and the heating turned off.
Call it Blitz spirit,
call him Churchill,
the dangling mayor,
flag in each hand
and a slur in his mouth.
Clap for carers,
3% for nurses,
lighten up.

He's got
the Sun in one pocket,
the Times in the other.
There's nothing a sobbing scapegoat won't solve,
not when he's got Cressida coming round for dinner.

Call him incompetent,
call for no confidence,

bang your fists,
take to Twitter,
rage and swear
and call him a liar,

then calm down,
go to bed.
You've had too much to drink;
you're embarrassing yourself,
dear.

I Stopped Drinking and Told Everyone I'd Been Given the Gift of Time

Spend it worrying that
perhaps that online careers test I did
in Year 8 which said I should be a lorry driver
was right.

All those PSHE lessons
on CVs and interview skills;
now I google the hourly rate of DPD drivers,
weigh it up against
paying off my student loan.

Before I knew what death was,
when I still counted down the days to my birthday,
I planned a life where I had six jobs:
dentist, vet, astronaut,
prime minister, ballet dancer,
poet.

Then everything became one long dad joke.
I just wanted to be the impoverished artist
swimming in baked beans and final demand letters,
knowing that my parents would never actually let me starve.
I spent a year planning my eighteenth,
drank half a bottle of tequila in forty-five minutes,
the next day couldn't remember any of it.

Now I only wish for a salary and Ocado shop,
imagine myself in an office with a headset.
I'm a woman who goes for bottomless brunch,
has weekends away with the girls from marketing
in Airbnbs with hot tubs.

Tell Us Your Trauma, but Remember to Use Similes

Can you personify the sound of the engine at
the border, the voice of the guard that was
too much like your father? Describe the barrel
you were placed in, how fast you ran, how
much you miss your sister; can you think of
a better title? *It's hard to describe, Miss.* Moved
across the world like a parcel with a smile, like
a shipment of faulty PPE. You missed a word
there; no broken English, please; give me all
your horror till the session's up.

He stands to switch the big light on, thinks
better of it, finds his coat and walks the flights
down to Tesco, spends ten minutes in front
of the glow of the fridge, grins at a security
guard who can't read his eyes over his mask.
Opens a tuna sweetcorn sandwich, walks for
an hour in each direction. Sudan to Derby city
centre. Placed in a tower block and told not to
move. Told to learn English, to speak it in our
shops, watch as people shrink from him, watch
as his future rolls out in front of him, watches James
Bond films on his phone, stays up all night Googling
what home looks like now, gets up at seven for an exam.
Changes the sheets and thinks of his mother. Shows
up early in the hope the teacher might unmute herself.

New Year's Resolution

imagine him

just back to the office
holding a hoisin duck Pret wrap
a packet of popcorn
lime and black pepper
he's taken the stairs
because it's the first week of January
checks his phone
as the double doors close
behind him
knows he can squeeze an episode
of *The Good Place* in
before his one o'clock meeting
crosses the office
remembers he should reply to his wife's text
about their daughter's one-to-one tuition
he sits in his swivel chair
tears open the plastic wrapper
turns forty-five degrees to his laptop screen
then Susan appears over the top of it
says

have you got a minute?

This Is What a Feminist Looks Like

Weinstein with the walking aid
geriatric Murdoch
stumbling old man shuffle

now this
ordinary Joe
English teacher
borrows a set of his mum's crutches
hobbles in clutching a fumbling pile of doctors' notes
they can't put him away
too fragile
and his family, Jesus
an anxious wife and two teenage children
they need him financially
shouldn't be punished
a sixteen-year-old daughter must be protected
at all costs
his precious baby girl
can't find out what he does to other people's
precious baby girls

he's sorry
for whatever this girl grown up
thinks
he may have
might not
maybe did
misremembers, obviously
too drunk
too sexy
bones running hot with dishonesty
not worth ruining a man's life over, surely?

one slip
but such a good clean record
society's gold standard upstanding member
makes a monthly direct debit to Women's Aid
when he remembers

THIS IS WHAT A FEMINIST LOOKS LIKE

his life too precious
too vital
his contribution too immeasurable
with so much left to give
what good could come from sticking him
amongst the other common criminals?

sure, you could make an example
of this pillar of the community
but what then?
where does it end?
this pillorying of men

witch hunts
fuelled by girls out for all
that they can get

and a police force
so relentlessly
on the side of women

Strip-lit Utopia

broken body clock car park
budget hotel and long-haul drivers
I put WhatsApp location on in case I'm murdered
and my husband has to find the body

I get my best worst ideas in service stations at 2am
cult TV scripts that'll be gone by morning
the Costa cashier doesn't look up
my face full of makeup   ears full of hoops
I want to tell her about my poorly attended gig
in a town hall between Burnley and Leeds
nothing to show but a back seat of books
two new Twitter followers and twenty quid

three hours to home
he's left my pyjamas on the laundry bin
save me clattering round in the dark

I check behind both seats before getting in
lock the doors
turn the heaters on
open a reduced cheese and onion sandwich
listen to a programme
on the history of the harmonium
let the windows fog

They Just Keep Going

for Leicester Rape Crisis

We arrive a cavalcade of teenage girls,
park outside the post office,
buy five packets of ready salted
in return for the key to the loo.

Our group,
a haze of eyelashes and pac-a-macs,
passed by men with walking poles and waterproofs.

We're not here for the miles
and by 2k I'm ready for stragglers,
but their bodies move them forward,
hands on tree trunks,
legs crouched over something disgusting,
squashed and skeletal.
Do you reckon a bird dropped it?

They're like tiny kids again,
buttercups under chins,
dandelion seed heads,
pink flowers
pressed into the pages of notebooks.

Is that corn, Miss?
Can we eat it?
Are we gonna see an eagle? Woodpecker? Pheasant?

No one complains about the drizzle and the heat
because out here no one wants anything from them,
no deadlines or pressure;
they're not being weighed up and measured.

It's not the run to the bus stop past the building site,
3am with keys between fingers,
or the corridor of boys with their phones out.

No long wait for a taxi that never comes,
no grades, no marks,
no scales, no mirrors,

these girls with their secrets
trying to keep it together,

just big skies
and trainer tread
on grass and gravel,
the promise
of a cheese cob picnic.

They just keep going

and at the end
as they lean against the minibus,
mouths full of flapjack,
the men come
with walking poles and waterproofs
and one of our gang says,
Have you been on the walk?
'Cause we have too.

Happy Birthday

as she cuts a piece of cake
passes it to her husband
unhappy about the direction the conversation has gone in
she says
some women just can't keep their knickers up

there is torn wrapping paper across the table
I have been asked to get on with this woman
this time
so I don't ask about her research
what studies she's citing
sources she's quoting
whether her evidence is qualitative or quantitative
what the variables were
over which time period
whether any placebos were involved
how the results were measured

which women
what knickers

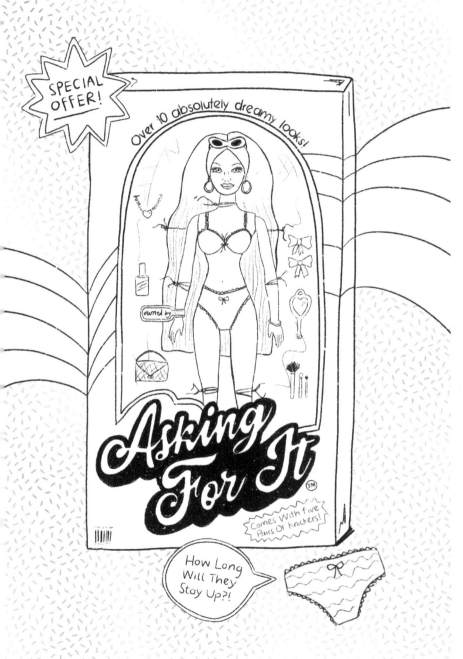

Gardening

she pays two hundred quid
to have them take her lawn away
lay astroturf instead
so when the dog shits she simply
has to bag it up and chuck it over the fence
no mowing, she crows
in the autumn she runs the hoover over
tells the neighbours
this stuff will outlive the apocalypse

she digs up the trees
to let in the light
covers beds in pebbles
to stop the weeds
sticks in bright plastic flowers
on spikes
they'll never die

fits tiny toy sparrows
that chirp like real
couple of felt squirrels
scatters a handful of rubber ants
across the path
puts down a sheet of shimmering glass
painted with lily pads

when the dog dies
it spurs her on to get rid of the cat

and before she leaves
for a fortnight in Center Parcs
she installs a mannequin
in the sun room
presses a pair of binoculars into its hands
turns out the light

Men

Our neighbour builds a home office in his garden,
invites his mates to try it
before it's finished, plastic sheeting
still whipping in the wind.
They arrive freshly shaved in cheap suits,
a parade of Range Rovers,
light cigarettes, admire his setup,
imagine themselves powerful,
securing contracts from the lawn.

A noughties indie playlist
through a speaker at an open window.
They order McDonald's,
throw wrappers over our fence.

At five they take off their ties,
stoke up the fire pit.
A wife brings a crate from the garage.
Their beer gut laughter carries over

to where my husband collects their litter
in crumpled t-shirt and sock feet,
then comes inside to start on dinner.

SOME COMMISSIONS

Enough Is Enough

for everyone I've knocked doors with in Leicester West

What is it that's going to make us snap?
For thirteen years we've watched them
systematically strip this country to scaffolding
and sell the best bits to their mates

and now the ground's unsteady,
the foundations are failing
and I don't know what it'll take
for us to demand our stability back.

Our NHS,
our welfare state,
our safety net
that always made this Britain great.

I grew up believing when someone slips
you hold them till they're back on their feet.
I grew up a child of the nineties,
a child of the Labour party.
I grew up knowing
you never trust a Tory
'cause all Tories know is greed.

Now every supermarket's got a foodbank bin
for you to put your kindness in
and energy's become a luxury
only available to the rich.

We are the frogs in the pot
and the water's reached boiling.
It's us versus them
and they've known this is coming
'cause there's only so long
they could keep us distracted
whilst they emptied the coffers.

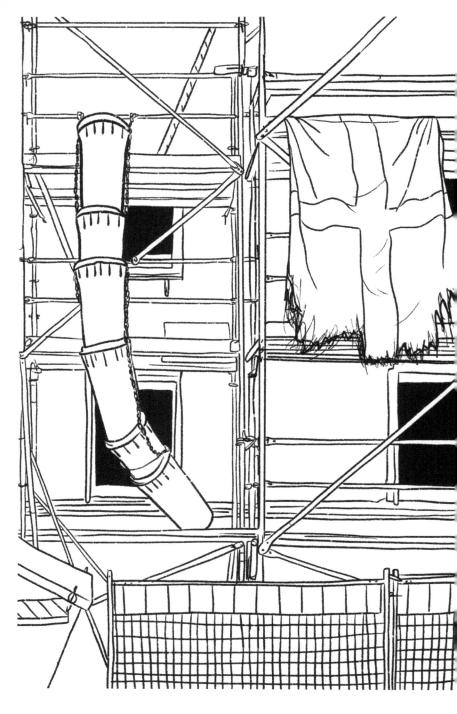

Whilst we fight each other for table scraps
they criminalise our placards
our right to speak,
to fill these streets
with voices asking for
some decency.

They have defunded our arts degrees,
told the kids to go get proper jobs
because nothing is more dangerous to them
than a whip-smart angry teenager
with a platform and a pen.

They tell us it'll trickle down
but meanwhile

we need to hug our pets,
batch cook porridge,
eat more soup
and cancel Netflix.

But watching Netflix never tanked the pound

and there's only so much you can blame
on Putin, Covid and Gordon Brown.

This is an island run by landlords and Murdoch,
whereas I was taught
it was meant to be run by us.

That's why they want us small,
they want us quiet,
they want us cold and hungry
with mould up the walls,

and whilst they partied through lockdown,
drank red wine till they were sick,

we remembered who we were
before someone opened the vault doors
and let the Tories take their pick.

We are a country of good people
run by the very worst
who've convinced us
that this scourge on the most vulnerable
is exactly what we deserve,

but it ends here,
you gluttonous vultures
on a decade-long smash and grab.

This is the straw that makes the country snap,
so give us what you took from us,
'cause now we want our country back.

Not Something That Other People Do

for Curve Theatre

it's not royal bones
below the place we used to park our cars
it's not the streets at a standstill
footballers on the bus
the trophy held up in Vicky Park
it's not knowing we've scored
from the roar of the crowd
over the canal
to my back garden
and it's definitely not
Benedict Cumberbatch
in the cathedral
reading a Carol Ann Duffy poem

(although it is
a bit)

it's a four-year-old looking up at a fifty-foot dinosaur
it's 2010's *X Factor* winner in the sold-out
Christmas pantomime at De Montfort Hall
it's a raucous audience at drag queen bingo
in a pub theatre off the Narborough Road

it's fear-free environments
anything goes
it's doing all the things you know your kids
would die from embarrassment from if they could see you now
but look at you go

it's unlocking a moment of joy in a silent child
a family learning how to play together
for the first time
it's the teenager finally finding a place
for all those feelings he so desperately didn't want you to see

it's illuminated stilt walkers
coffee shop basements
neon lights on dusky skylines
howling, roaring pin-sharp acoustics
polished brass and remorseless steam

it's not saying *art for all* because it ticks a funding box
gets you a nice review in *the Guardian*
it's for the people who don't even want art
stick two fingers up to art
and say, *what's art ever done for me?*
for the people who wouldn't know where to begin with art
where do you even find art?
because art was the teacher who told me I couldn't draw
and sent me to sit in the corridor for two hours
instead of doing art

it is not over there
not on the other side
not something that other people do
it's not right or wrong
not only if you speak in the correct language
agree with us
read the notes before attending the session

it's not only if you can successfully navigate the networking event
too-small teacup clattering through the
skin-crawlingly awkward chitchat

it's not fifty quid
it's not only in London
it's not *did you hear that programme about it on Radio 4?*
no, I did not
it's not *have you read Chekhov?*
although sometimes it is
and that's fine
for those guys
who like Chekhov
they are welcome here too

but it is in you
and it is messy and stupid
and rude
and delicate and precious
and if you feel it
then feed it
and bring it to us

because we are an island of red
in an ocean of blue
we are swimming against the tide
when four million children live below the poverty line

we are not giving up
when it feels too tough
when all the fight's gone out of us
with fewer and fewer schools having the time
or the cash
to teach creativity in their classrooms
that's when we pick up the slack
plug the growing gap
between the haves
and the cannot-afford-tos

in these dangerous and difficult times
when freedom of expression
has never felt so threatened
we open our arms wider
we have enough space at our tables
we want to hear your stories
so write them down
play them out
on our stages
in our studios

we are well used to playing the underdog here
and here we leave no one behind

we build our communities
on the rare belief that art is a fundamental right
the great leveller that lifts all
from Clarendon Park to Belgrave Road

we know
that success is no accident
it begins with a moment
and grows with the relentless cultivation of talent

you don't have to be an unremitting extrovert to join this
there is no club to sign up to
no clique to hang out with
we just need you
it is OK to switch off the news for an evening
we feel it too
so bring us your fears
your dreams and your heartbreak
take a break from it all for a bit

there is a door here
a seat
a ticket

the world is raging outside
so come in
give us your time
and together we might just change it

Sequins and Solidarity

for Eurovision

come in
it's 1956 and we are a continent in recovery
what better than a song, then
a game, a contest
grab your gladrags
and black tie finery
or just your slippers
your mates, your mum
the kids, the dog
stick the telly on

for this international experiment
united by music and recent history

now just shy of seventy years on
we're Europe's most raucous election
glitterball referendum
Tallinn to Bilbao
all here, now
your name's on the door
and all are welcome on these phoenix rising shores

come shimmy in our rich biography of underdogs and everyone
all voices will be heard on this floor
all dance moves applauded
at our shimmering festival
that's stood tall over Europe's history
orchestra pit to DJ decks
black and white to strobe lights
watched while the Berlin wall came down
and the party doubled in size

there are no borders in this contest
just spotlit snapshots
postcards across continents

a baton passed
a trophy carried
and this year we are the bittersweet caretakers
of our displaced guests of honour

what better than a song, then
a dance
a party
joyful resistance
one great bass-pumping
act of rebellion
tonight we will sing
with our arms around strangers
jive around pubs
boogie on sofas
wear flags like capes
root for the opposition
learn eighteen different ways
to say music

while it rages outside
in here we are twirling, unified and fearless

so tomorrow when the sun rises
the air still full of sax solos and top notes
left amongst the empty glasses
rubble and dust
will be the unmistakeable echoes of hope

Semper Eadem

for Leicester Museum

traditionless city
no accent at all community
with our skyline of church spires and minarets
streets of cobblestones and Roman baths
and all that history lost to the ring road

it's not utopia
this landlocked island
we're not always pretty
but we're scrappy
and we're welcoming
quietly radical underdogs
when even our motto is underwhelming
always the same
consistently resilient
non-conformist metropolis of dissent

with our hard-won tolerance
history of repeatedly seeing off the National Front
putting them on the first bus back to where they came from
with a quiet confidence
we're identifiable by all the things we're not
not Northern
not Coventry, Derby or Nottingham

we're uni halls and terraced streets
council estates and red brick semis

we're foreign tongues and mother tongues
the teacher on the school gate welcoming kids
in thirteen different tongues

we're no longer gloves and shoes
shirts and garters
but curry and jewellery
crisps and samosas

food done properly
a national curiosity

twenty-two countries in one stretch of high street
cheek by jowl
we're shopkeepers trading services for favours
a parallel currency of clean windows for free lunches

we're cathedral bells
and Friday prayers
football chants
and market traders

we're home when home is no longer an option
home because it's always been home
because your granddad got one of the first houses
on the Eyres Monsell
and still has the original flooring
we're home because of an advert in the *Ugandan Argus*
because of Windrush
because of war
because of fleeing
because we rub along pretty well
all of us

residents and visitors
travellers and friends

the crowd of forty thousand wrapped up in big coats
with sweet tea and barfi on Belgrave Road
outside the town hall in reindeer ears and Santa hats,
scores of mothers and daughters
at the unveiling of Alice Hawkins
always and always facing towards the light

we're hot dogs at the race course on Bonfire Night

the warmth of comedy gigs in the middle of winter
school sports day at Saffron Lane
Summer Sundae and Simon Says
the Big Session
the Cookie, Charlotte and Musician
we're Kasabian's homecoming gig
and all the stages in every theatre this city's ever seen

we're Jamie Vardy in the Premier League
our inexplicable Statue of Liberty
2am McDonald's on Market Street
when we just piled out of Fan Club
New Walk when it snows
and the street lights make it feel like Narnia

we're peregrines
the tiny train in Abbey Park
canoes on the canal
nurses and factory workers
to and from shifts along the towpath

every playground and the unwritten rule
that if you can't speak the language
but you can kick a ball
or play cricket
then you're in

this understated middle place
that talks itself down given half a chance
and has trouble knowing what to put on its postcards

come for the car park king
stay for Ranieri

but we're more than Adrian Mole
more than Gary Lineker
and a half-decent jalfrezi

we're the feeling of belonging
the space we make for each other
each new arrival
new community
the way we all shuffle up a bit

the way we don't shout about it
semper eadem   always the same
this traditionless, accentless
city.

FINALLY,

Invitation

I text you from my office
overlooking the street
ten minutes before a meeting with an exec
I'm in slippers, have a hot water bottle
stuffed up the back of my jumper
my notebook, a cheap, one-pound
thing from Sainsbury's
is empty

you're fifteen years ago
in low-rise jeans and lace knickers
it's only a Thursday afternoon
but you're in the Loaded Dog
drinking wine as fast as the boys drink cider

you all have to be back in class in twenty minutes
but you had an offer to study Creative Writing in Liverpool
last week and have fancied yourself
Seamus Heaney ever since

too busy playing pool and Tuesday nights in Fan Club
to bother with actually reading anything
but having been given ten minutes at an open mic
you're convinced you're the greatest writer that ever lived

you reply quickly on your Nokia 3210
anything to avoid double Psychology
who needs it anyway, where you're headed

so here you are drunk and loud beside me
purple hair and belly button piercing
laying your confidence across my desk
as the exec asks what I'm working on
at the moment

there's a silence
you glance pitifully at the date written neatly

across the top of my page
and pull out your own notebook
moleskin, covered in stickers of bands
that boys you fancy play in
I recognise it as one of hundreds
now up in the loft
you part the pages with the silk divider
and without being asked
descend into the first stanza
of a poem you wrote on the bus
on the way here

afterwards, you admire my bookshelves
notice the ones with your name on
show posters and slam trophies
you take a second look at me
in my charity shop jumper
and unbrushed teeth
I don't show you the inbox of rejections
dwindling bank balance
social media
a party of everyone who's doing better than you

instead, I take you to dinner
with my husband's family
you look at the man you'll marry
listen to people asking me again what it is I do for a living
only for them to talk over me
about their jobs in insurance and accountancy
and as they wring their hands
over what to do with all that money
you reach across the table
top up my glass
and tell me to speak up

16th March 2023

Credits

'They Just Keep Going' was written for a project with Slow Ways and Leicester Rape Crisis, August 2023.

'Enough Is Enough' was written for the Leicester Enough is Enough Protests, October 2022.

'Not Something That Other People Do' was commissioned by Curve Theatre in 2020.

'Sequins and Solidarity' was commissioned by the BBC and produced by BBC Studios for The Eurovision Song Contest 2023 which was held in Liverpool.

'Semper Eadem' was commissioned by Leicester City Council for the Leicester Stories Gallery at Leicester Museum & Art Gallery, 2021